SENSATIONAL SUMMER FOOD

D1823728

As the days grow longer and warmer, meals start to move out of the dining room and onto the patio, or are taken in a picnic hamper to a favourite spot in the countryside or by the water. With these ideas in mind, the dishes that can be prepared quickly and that release you from standing over a hot kitchen stove are the ones you turn to most often.

So, to start with, we have a chapter full of recipes that are all light and easy to prepare. Recipes such as, Focaccia Heroes and Toasted Alligators, can be quickly assembled when the teenagers are ransacking the fridge for a snack, and others, like the Tomato Dill Soup, can be prepared in the cool of the evening in readiness for lunch the next day. The next chapter contains recipes for dishes that either need no cooking at all, or which can be cooked beforehand and served cold. Some wonderful salads are included – the Lamb and Pepper Salad is a great way to use up any left-over roast lamb.

Make this the summer when your picnic hamper is the one everyone envies. Some of the dishes, especially the delicious Rabbit Pistachio Terrine, may take a little time to prepare, but there's certainly no excuse for boring old egg sandwiches again! If you are a guest at a picnic, then take along some freshly baked Olive Herb Bread or a Cinnamon Picnic Cake – you will be sure to be invited again.

Our final chapter features some wonderful recipes for that enjoyable occasion known as The Long Summer Lunch. Some of the dishes, such as Avocados with Julienne Salad, Poached Salmon with Mango Mint Sauce, and Tropical Fruit Fondue, have been designed to go together as a complete menu, but you can cook only as much as you feel inclined to. After all, it's your turn to relax, too!

CONTENTS

LIGHT AND EASY

Cool soups, toasted sandwiches and other easily prepared snacks are perfect for those times when hungry teenagers have a snack attack or you just want something simple yet tasty for an impromptu weekend brunch. You're sure to find something that will fit the bill perfectly amongst this selection of satisfying recipes.

Bagel Thins

2 bagels, cut in 2 from top to bottom

1 tblspn unsalted butter, melted

1 tspn chopped fresh oregano

1 tspn chopped fresh basil

1 Preheat oven to 180°C (350°F/ Gas 4). Using a sharp serrated knife, slice bagel halves into very thin slices. Place on a baking sheet in 1 layer. Brush with butter and sprinkle with herbs.

2 Bake for 10-12 minutes. Cool, then store in an airtight container.

Serves 4

Bruschetta

1 loaf Italian bread

125ml (4fl oz) light olive oil

2-3 cloves garlic, peeled and cut in half

2 large ripe, firm tomatoes, diced

2 spring onions, finely sliced

6 basil leaves, chopped

2 tblspn balsamic vinegar or white vinegar

1 tspn freshly ground black pepper

1 Cut loaf into 2cm (³/4in) slices. Brush olive oil on both sides of slices then rub with garlic. Place under a preheated medium grill and toast both sides until golden.

2 Mix tomatoes with spring onions and basil, add vinegar and black pepper and lightly toss. Heap spoonfuls of tomato mixture onto bread slices and serve immediately.

Serves 8

Spicy Meatballs

90g (3oz) sultanas

500g (1lb) lean minced lamb

2 tblspn pine nuts

1 small onion, finely chopped

1 tblspn chopped fresh parsley

1 clove garlic, crushed

1 tspn ground cumin

1 tspn ground cinnamon

assorted fresh vegetables for dipping

Bagel Thins to serve, see recipe this page

Coriander Sauce

200g (6¹/2oz) natural yogurt

1 clove garlic, crushed

3 tblspn fresh coriander leaves

1 Preheat oven to 200°C (400°F/ Gas 6). Soak sultanas in hot water for 15 minutes, drain and chop coarsely. Combine sultanas, lamb, pine nuts, onion, parsley, garlic, cumin and cinnamon in a bowl and mix well. Shape mixture into 25 balls and place in a single layer on an ungreased baking sheet. Bake, uncovered, for 30 minutes or until cooked through.

2 Combine sauce ingredients and let stand for 30 minutes. Serve meatballs hot or cold with dipping sauce, vegetables and Bagel Thins.

Serves 4-6

Spicy Meatballs platter with Coriander Sauce, Bagel Thins and Bruschetta

Tomato Dill Soup

2-3 tblspn light olive oil

2 large onions, peeled and sliced

2 cloves garlic, crushed

1 handful fresh dill, finely chopped

salt

freshly ground black pepper

1.5 litres (2½pt) chicken stock

1.5kg (3lb) tomatoes, coarsely chopped

pinch of sugar

2 tspn finely grated orange rind

dill sprigs and diced cucumber for garnish

1 Heat oil in a large saucepan, add onions and cook gently for 20 minutes or until tender and lightly coloured. Add garlic and cook for a further 3-5 minutes. Place dill with salt and black pepper to taste to pan and cook for 15 minutes. Add chicken stock, tomatoes and sugar. Bring to the boil, reduce heat, cover and simmer for 30 minutes.

2 Push the soup through a sieve. Add orange rind and set aside to cool. Chill for several hours or overnight before serving.

3 Taste and check for seasoning – it may need more after chilling. Ladle soup into bowls and garnish with dill or cucumber.

Serves 4

Herbed Soda Bread

315g (10oz) wholemeal flour

250g (8oz) plain flour

2 tspn salt

2 tspn sugar

1 tspn bicarbonate of soda

¾ tspn baking powder

90g (3oz) butter

30g (1oz) chopped fresh parsley

1 tblspn snipped fresh chives

1 tblspn chopped fresh rosemary or 1 tspn dried rosemary

500ml (16fl oz) buttermilk

1 Preheat oven to 190°C (375°F/ Gas 5). Sift the flours, salt, sugar, bicarbonate of soda and baking powder into a large bowl. Rub in butter with fingertips until mixture resembles breadcrumbs. Stir in herbs, add buttermilk and mix to make a soft dough.

2 Place dough onto a greased baking sheet and, with floured hands, shape into a 20cm (8in) round. Using a sharp, floured knife, cut a cross, 1cm (½in) deep, in the top.

3 Bake for 40-50 minutes or until loaf sounds hollow when tapped on the base. Serve warm or at room temperature, sliced.

Serves 6

Tomato Dill Soup

Plate Accoutrement

Herbed Soda Bread, Chilled Butternut Soup

Chilled Butternut Soup

1 onion, sliced

60g (2oz) butter

750g (1¹/₂lb) butternut pumpkin, chopped

4 thin slices lemon, seeds removed

30g (1oz) plain flour

1.5 litres (2¹/₂pt) warm chicken stock

salt

freshly ground white pepper

250ml (8fl oz) double cream, chilled

lemon juice to taste

chopped fresh chives for garnish

1 Cook onion gently in butter in a large saucepan until soft. Stir in pumpkin and lemon slices, sprinkle with flour and stir over low heat for 3 minutes. Remove from heat and cool a little, then add chicken stock, stirring until blended.

2 Return to heat and bring to the boil, stirring constantly. Season lightly with salt and white pepper and simmer, partially covered, for 30 minutes. Discard lemon slices. Purée mixture in a blender or food processor and pour into a bowl. Allow to cool, then chill, covered, for at least 4 hours.

3 Stir in chilled cream and lemon juice. Adjust seasonings and serve in chilled bowls sprinkled with chives.

Serves 6-8

Cheese Stratas

1 tblspn French mustard

8 slices square white bread trimmed to fit ramekins

8 spring onions, finely sliced

1 tblspn butter

8 slices Cheddar cheese or a mixture of Cheddar and Swiss cheeses

2 eggs, beaten

500ml (16fl oz) hot milk

2 tblspn finely chopped fresh parsley

¹/₄ tspn salt

pinch each cayenne pepper and paprika

1 Preheat oven to 180°C (350°F/ Gas 4). Grease 4 individual ovenproof dishes or ramekins. Spread mustard over one side of bread slices. Sauté spring onions in butter for 2-3 minutes or until soft. Arrange alternate layers of bread, onions and cheese in prepared dishes, ending with a layer of cheese. Combine remaining ingredients and slowly pour over bread layers.

2 Place dishes in a shallow baking tin with enough hot water to come halfway up sides of dishes and bake for 25 minutes or until puffy and just set.

Serves 4

Mexican Munchies

250g (8oz) cream cheese

2 cloves garlic, crushed

125g (4oz) sour cream

1 large avocado, mashed

1 tspn lemon juice

1 tomato, seeded and chopped

1 tspn chilli paste

4 bacon rashers, diced and fried until crisp

3 spring onions, finely sliced

1 medium red or green pepper, finely chopped

170ml (5$1/2$fl oz) hot taco sauce

125g (4oz) mature Cheddar cheese, grated

1 Place cream cheese, garlic and sour cream in a food processor and process until combined. Spread mixture over base of a 23cm (9in) pie plate or other shallow dish. Mix the avocado, lemon juice, tomato and chilli paste in a small bowl.

2 Spread avocado mixture over the cream cheese layer. Sprinkle on the bacon, spring onion and red or green pepper. Pour taco sauce over top and sprinkle with cheese. Serve with corn chips.

Serves 4-6

Toasted Alligators

1 French bread stick, halved lengthwise

3 tblspn butter

fruit chutney

155g (5oz) mortadella or salami, thinly sliced

2 tomatoes, sliced

90g (3oz) Jarlsberg or Cheddar cheese, thinly sliced

6 anchovy fillets

6 black olives, chopped, or stuffed olives, sliced

freshly ground black pepper

1 Toast bread stick, crusty-sides-up, under a preheated medium grill until golden.

2 Spread untoasted surfaces with butter, then chutney. Cover bottom half of bread with mortadella or salami, tomatoes, and cheese, folding slices if too large. Scatter with anchovies and olives and grill until cheese is bubbly. Season with black pepper to taste.

3 Top loaf with remaining half and press down well. Cut diagonally into 3 or 4 lengths and serve.

Serves 3-4

Green Bean Roll-Ups

410g (13oz) stringless green beans, trimmed

2 tomatoes, diced

2 tblspn cider vinegar

2 tblspn light olive oil

2 tspn Dijon mustard

2 tspn sugar

1 clove garlic, crushed

3 tblspn snipped fresh chives

1 tspn freshly ground black pepper

8 whole lettuce leaves or 4 pitta breads

1 Boil, steam or microwave beans until just tender. Rinse under cold water, drain well and chill.

2 Combine tomatoes, vinegar, oil, mustard, sugar, garlic, chives and black pepper in a small bowl and mix well. Chill thoroughly.

3 Spoon tomato mixture over beans, then place a portion in each lettuce leaf and roll up, or halve pitta breads, toast on both sides and tuck bean mixture into pockets.

Serves 8

Cheese and Spinach Turnovers

250g (8oz) feta cheese, chopped

45g (1$1/2$oz) finely chopped spinach leaves

3 tblspn chopped fresh parsley

1 tblspn chopped fresh mint

1 onion, finely chopped

2 tblspn lemon juice

2 eggs, beaten

$1/2$ tspn nutmeg

salt

freshly ground black pepper

375g (12oz) prepared puff or flaky pastry

1 Place all ingredients except pastry and only half of the eggs in a bowl and thoroughly mix to combine. Roll out pastry to a 30cm (12in) square and cut into 8 squares. Divide filling among the squares, mounding it on one triangular half to leave a 2cm ($3/4$in) margin.

2 Brush pastry edges with some remaining egg and fold over to make triangles, pressing edges together with a fork to seal. Place on lightly greased baking sheets and chill for 20 minutes.

3 Preheat oven to 220°C (425°F/Gas 7). Brush turnovers with remaining egg and cut a small slit in top of each. Bake for 8-10 minutes or until pastry begins to colour. Reduce heat to 180°C (350°F/Gas 4) and bake for 15 minutes more, covering turnovers loosely with foil if pastry browns too quickly.

Serves 4

Focaccia Heroes

Focaccia Heroes

1 clove garlic, crushed

2 tblspn butter, softened

1 large piece focaccia (enough for 4)

16 slices hot Italian salami or 4 slices ham

2 tomatoes, sliced

1 red onion, finely sliced

1 red pepper, seeded and sliced

4 pinches fresh oregano

4 slices Jarslberg cheese

1 Mash garlic into softened butter until combined. Cut focaccia into 4 equal pieces. Slice each piece in half horizontally and spread with butter mixture. Divide remaining ingredients equally on top of focaccia bases, ending with the cheese.

2 Place both filled and empty focaccia halves under a preheated hot grill until the cheese is melted and bread is brown. Replace top halves and serve warm.

Serves 4

Coconut and Curry Calamari

60g (2oz) self-raising flour

90ml (3fl oz) water

60ml (2fl oz) coconut milk

1 egg, lightly beaten

75g (2¹/₂oz) shredded coconut

750g (1¹/₂lb) calamari rings, cleaned

90g (3oz) cornflour

vegetable oil for deep-frying

Curry Mayonnaise

250g (8oz) egg mayonnaise

2 tblspn fruit chutney

2 tspn curry powder

1 tblspn lemon juice

1 tblspn tomato purée

1 Sift flour into a bowl, make a well in the centre. Add water, coconut milk, egg and shredded coconut and gradually mix to make a smooth batter.

2 Heat oil in a saucepan until a cube of bread dropped in browns in 50 seconds. Toss calamari rings in cornflour to coat and shake off excess. Dip into batter, briefly drain and deep-fry, a few at a time, until golden brown.

3 Mix together thoroughly all ingredients for the mayonnaise and serve with calamari.

Serves 4

Smoked Salmon Open Sandwiches

fresh dill sprigs, chilled

watercress or lettuce leaves

6 slices rye or black bread, buttered

6-8 slices smoked salmon

6 slices lemon for garnish

125g (4oz) sour cream

Place dill and watercress or lettuce leaves on buttered bread. Fold salmon slices and place on top. Garnish with lemon slices and dollops of sour cream.

Serves 6

Avocado and Bacon Sandwich

1 ripe avocado, halved and stoned

2 slices wholegrain toast, buttered

5-6 small lettuce leaves

1 tomato, sliced

salt

freshly ground black pepper

1½ tblspn vinaigrette dressing, optional

2 large bacon rashers, rind removed

1 Peel avocado and thickly slice. Place each slice of toast on a plate and arrange lettuce, tomato and avocado on top. Season to taste with salt and black pepper and a little vinaigrette (if using).

2 Cut bacon into strips, cook in a dry frying pan on moderate heat until browned. Tip bacon and hot dripping over sandwiches and serve immediately.

Serves 2

Tuna Melts

250g (8oz) canned tuna in brine, drained

1 stalk celery, finely sliced

2 spring onions, finely sliced

60g (2oz) mayonnaise

4 slices thick bread

15g (½oz) alfalfa sprouts

4 slices Emmenthal or Jarlsberg cheese

1 Mix tuna, celery, spring onions and mayonnaise in a small bowl. Place bread under preheated medium grill and toast on one side only.

2 Spread one-quarter of the tuna mixture on untoasted side of each bread slice and top with one-quarter of the sprouts and one slice of cheese. Return to grill and heat until cheese melts.

Serves 4

The BLT

3-4 bacon rashers, rind removed

2 slices white bread

2 tblspn mayonnaise

4 slices tomato

salt

1 crisp lettuce leaf

1 Fry bacon until crisp and drain on paper towels. Toast bread and spread each slice with mayonnaise.

2 Pile tomatoes on one slice, season with salt to taste and top with bacon, lettuce and second slice of toast, mayonnaise-side-down. Serve immediately.

Serves 1

Avocado and Bacon Sandwich

Bratwurst Rolls

4 long soft bread rolls

butter, melted

6 spring onions, finely chopped

3-4 tblspn chopped mixed fresh herbs, or
4-5 tblspn chopped fresh parsley with
1 tspn dried mixed herbs

4 hot grilled bratwurst or similar Continental
sausages

Dijon mustard

salt

freshly ground black pepper

1 Slit rolls lengthwise and pull out some of the centres from each side. Brush insides with butter and sprinkle with spring onions and herbs.

2 Split sausages lengthwise, spread insides generously with mustard and close up. Place a sausage in each hollowed roll (trim to fit, if necessary), season to taste with salt and black pepper and press roll back together. Wrap in foil and refrigerate up to several hours or overnight.

3 Preheat oven to 180°C (350°F/ Gas 4). Heat rolls, still in foil straight from the refrigerator, for 20 minutes. Unwrap for the last 2 minutes to crispen.

Serves 4

Roast Beef on French Bread

4 x 12cm (5in) lengths of French bread,
split horizontally leaving the halves attached

125g (4oz) blue vein cheese, rind
discarded

45g (1¹/₂oz) watercress sprigs

500g (1lb) thinly sliced rare roast beef

60g (2oz) mayonnaise

1 tblspn drained, bottled horseradish

salt

freshly ground black pepper

1 Open bread pieces, spread cut sides with blue vein cheese, top with watercress sprigs and beef slices.

2 In a bowl, combine the mayonnaise and horseradish and drizzle over beef. Season sandwiches with salt and black pepper to taste and close them, pressing firmly.

Serves 4

French Bread Tartare

1 long French bread stick

90g (3oz) butter, softened

1 large clove garlic, crushed

375g (12oz) lean steak, finely minced

1 egg, beaten

1 tspn salt

¹/₂ tspn freshly ground black pepper

6 spring onions, finely chopped (include
some green tops)

2 tblspn finely chopped capers

dash Worcestershire sauce

1 Preheat oven to 200°C (400°F/Gas 6). Cut loaf in half lengthwise and scoop out centres. Combine butter and garlic and spread over insides of the bread halves. Place loaf, cut-side-up, on a baking sheet and bake for 5 minutes or until golden.

2 Mix remaining ingredients together and taste for seasoning. Fill the bottom half of the loaf with steak mixture and press top half back into place. Wrap tightly in foil and chill for 2 hours. Cut into thin slices to serve.

Serves 6

Chicken Club

4 slices lean bacon

2 boneless chicken breast fillets

freshly ground black pepper

12 thick slices white or brown bread cut
from large round or rectangular loaves,
toasted lightly

125g (4oz) mayonnaise

8 lettuce leaves, rinsed and dried

8 thin slices tomato

8 thin slices red onion

1 Place bacon in a small heavy frying pan and cook until crisp. Drain on paper towels reserving 1 tablespoon fat in pan.

2 Add fillets to pan, season with pepper to taste and cook for 5-6 minutes on each side or until just tender. Drain and set chicken aside to cool for 10 minutes, then cut into thin slices.

3 Spread 1 side each of 4 slices of toast with mayonnaise and sprinkle with black pepper to taste. Add a lettuce leaf and 1 slice each of tomato, onion and bacon. Place another slice of toast on top and add another lettuce leaf and slice of onion, tomato and chicken. Finish with another slice of toast, and press together firmly. Cut sandwiches diagonally in half. If liked, secure with toothpicks topped with stuffed olives.

Serves 4

Smoked Cheese and Roasted Pepper Rolls

8 black olives, pitted

1 tblspn lemon juice

60ml (2fl oz) olive oil

¹/₂ clove garlic

cayenne pepper

4 x 10cm (4in) lengths Italian bread,
halved horizontally

1 large red pepper, roasted and quartered

250g (8oz) smoked cheese, thinly sliced

45g (1¹/₂oz) fresh basil leaves

Clockwise from top left: Bratwurst Rolls, Roast Beef on French Bread, Chicken Club, Smoked Cheese and Roasted Pepper Rolls, Salad and Basil on Cottage Bread

1 In a blender or food processor, process olives, lemon juice, oil, garlic and cayenne pepper to taste until smooth. Brush cut sides of bread with mixture.

2 Divide roasted pepper, cheese and basil between bread bases. Replace the top halves and press sandwiches together firmly.

Serves 4

Kitchen Tip

To roast pepper, pierce with a fork and char the skin almost black and blistered over a gas flame, or under a preheated grill, turning often, for 15 minutes. Place in a paper bag and let stand until cool enough to handle. Peel off skin and discard ribs and seeds.

Salad and Basil on Cottage Bread

125g (4oz) mayonnaise

1 tspn curry powder, or to taste

8 slices of country-style bread or cottage loaf

2 firm tomatoes, sliced

1 Lebanese cucumber, peeled if desired and thinly sliced diagonally

1 red onion, thinly sliced

fresh basil leaves

salt

freshly ground black pepper

15g (1/2oz) fresh mint leaves

1 In a small bowl, combine mayonnaise and curry powder. Spread mixture on 1 side of each slice of bread.

2 Top half the bread slices with tomatoes, cucumber, onion and basil. Sprinkle with salt and black pepper to taste and add mint. Top sandwiches with remaining bread slices. Press together firmly.

Serves 4

KEEP IT COOL

There are many times during the summer months when you want to be able to serve a meal that's not heavy yet is more than a snack, that either needs little cooking or, better still, no cooking at all! It's for those occasions that we put these recipes together – lots of interesting salads and some scrumptious fruity desserts.

Vitello Tonnato

1-1.5kg (2-3lb) boneless veal joint, firmly tied

1 carrot

1 stalk celery

1 onion, quartered

handful of parsley sprigs

1 small bay leaf

lemon slices, whole capers and parsley or watercress for garnish

Tuna Sauce

200g (6¹/₂oz) canned tuna in oil, undrained

5 anchovy fillets

185ml (6fl oz) olive oil

3 tblspn lemon juice

3 tblspn capers

315g (10oz) mayonnaise

1 Place veal, carrot, celery, onion, parsley and bay leaf in a large saucepan with just enough water to cover veal. Bring slowly to the boil, cover and simmer gently for 2 hours. Remove from heat and leave meat to cool in liquid.

2 To make sauce, place tuna, anchovies, olive oil, lemon juice and capers in a blender or food processor and process until creamy. Transfer to a bowl and fold in mayonnaise.

3 Remove string from veal and cut into thin, neat slices. Spread a thin layer of sauce on a serving dish and arrange a single layer of veal slices on top. Spread more sauce over veal and top with another thin layer of slices. Continue layering remaining sauce and veal, reserving a little sauce for a final coat at serving time. Cover veal with plastic food wrap and refrigerate for several hours or overnight.

4 Before serving, spread with reserved sauce and garnish with lemon slices, capers and parsley or watercress.
Serves 8

Portuguese Tuna Pâté

200g (6¹/₂oz) canned tuna in oil, drained

125g (4oz) butter, diced

60ml (2fl oz) double cream

¹/₂ tspn dry mustard

¹/₄ tspn cayenne pepper, or to taste

60ml (2fl oz) Madeira or dry sherry

salt

freshly ground white pepper

lemon slices and parsley sprigs for garnish

Melba toast to serve

1 Place tuna in a blender or food processor. With machine running, add butter, cream, mustard, cayenne and madeira or sherry, and process until smooth. Season to taste.

2 Spoon pâté into a serving bowl or into 4 individual ramekins. Smooth the top, cover and chill until firm. Garnish with lemon and parsley and serve with Melba toast.
Serves 4

Kitchen Tip
To make Melba toast, preheat oven to 150°C (300°F/Gas 2). Toast sliced bread lightly on both sides then trim off crusts and slice each piece, while still warm, through the soft middle to make two very thin pieces. Cut each piece into 4 triangles and place in one layer on a baking sheet. Bake until dried, crisp and curled. Cool and store airtight.

Vitello Tonnato

Bacon Mushroom Salad

500g (1lb) spinach

500g (1lb) rocket or 250g (8oz) watercress

1 red onion, finely sliced

250g (8oz) button mushrooms, finely sliced

250g (8oz) bacon, cut into large cubes

2 hard-boiled eggs, sliced

45g (1¹/₂oz) sesame seeds, toasted

Balsamic Vinegar Dressing

2 tblspn balsamic vinegar or red wine vinegar

salt

freshly ground black pepper

60ml (2fl oz) walnut or hazelnut oil

60ml (2fl oz) light olive oil

1 To make dressing, mix vinegar with salt and black pepper to taste in a small bowl. Whisk in oils gradually until thickened.

2 Wash spinach and rocket, trim stems and dry. Tear greens into bite-sized pieces and place in a salad bowl, add onion and mushrooms and toss to combine.

3 Cook bacon in a dry frying pan until crisp and drain on paper towels. Pour dressing over salad and toss well. Sprinkle with bacon, eggs and sesame seeds and serve.

Serves 6-8

Lamb and Pepper Salad

1 green pepper, thinly sliced

1 red pepper, thinly sliced

3 spring onions, chopped

500g (1lb) cold roast lamb, cut into strips

1 tblspn French mustard

1 tblspn wine vinegar

2 tspn soy sauce

60ml (2fl oz) olive oil

3 tblspn chopped fresh parsley

salt

freshly ground black pepper

4 pitta breads, halved crosswise

1 Place red and green pepper, spring onions and lamb in a bowl.

2 Combine mustard, vinegar and soy sauce in a small bowl. Slowly whisk in the oil until thickened. Add parsley and season to taste. Toss mixture with salad and serve in pitta pockets.

Serves 4

Bacon and Mushroom Salad

Pasta with Spinach and Tomatoes

Green Pasta and Seafood Salad

350g (11oz) spinach tagliatelle

410g (13oz) canned chunk tuna in brine

2 small onions, finely sliced

3 ripe tomatoes, peeled and quartered

2 hard-boiled eggs, quartered

handful black olives, stoned

chopped fresh parsley for garnish

Vinaigrette Dressing

2 tblspn wine vinegar

1 tspn French mustard

6 tblspn virgin olive oil

salt

freshly ground black pepper

1 Cook pasta following package directions until *al dente*. Drain well and set aside to cool.

2 In a large bowl, flake tuna with a fork, add pasta, onions, tomatoes, eggs and olives and lightly toss to combine.

3 To make dressing, whisk together vinegar and mustard until combined. Add salt and black pepper to taste, then olive oil, a little at a time, whisking constantly until thickened. Spoon dressing over salad, toss lightly to coat and garnish with parsley.

Serves 6

Pasta with Spinach and Tomatoes

300g (9¹/₂oz) pasta shapes such as shells, penne or fusilli

1 tblspn balsamic vinegar

500g (1lb) spinach, washed and torn into pieces

250g (8oz) cherry tomatoes, halved

1 roasted red pepper, cut into strips

1 red onion, diced

2 tblspn drained capers

90g (3oz) Kalamata olives, halved and pitted

handful fresh basil leaves, cut into strips

Red Pepper Dressing

125ml (4fl oz) olive oil

1 clove garlic, crushed

pinch red pepper flakes

salt

freshly ground black pepper

1 To make dressing, combine oil, garlic, red pepper flakes, salt and pepper to taste in a small bowl and set aside.

2 Cook pasta following package directions for 10-12 minutes or until *al dente*. Drain well, transfer to a large bowl and toss with the dressing and vinegar, adding a little more oil or vinegar to taste. Set aside to cool.

3 Add spinach, tomatoes, roasted pepper, onion, capers, olives and basil to pasta and lightly toss to combine. Season to taste with salt and black pepper and serve at room temperature.

Serves 6

Potato and Watercress Salad

1kg (2lb) new potatoes

250ml (8fl oz) dry white wine

500g (1lb) watercress

3 hard-boiled eggs, chopped

1 tblspn chopped fresh parsley

Mustard Dressing

6 tblspn olive oil

1 tspn Dijon mustard

2 tblspn wine vinegar

salt

freshly ground black pepper

1 Cook potatoes in boiling salted water until just tender, drain and cut into slices while still warm. Place potatoes in a bowl and sprinkle with wine, tossing gently (the potatoes will absorb the wine).

2 Wash watercress, break off end branches and tie in bundles. Place in water until required.

3 When ready to serve, shake excess water off watercress and add to potatoes. Mix all dressing ingredients together, pour over salad and toss gently. Arrange salad in a dome-shape on serving platter and sprinkle with combined egg and parsley.

Serves 8

Salad Japonaise

2 lettuce hearts such as cos, butterhead or iceberg

1 small pineapple, peeled and cubed or sliced

1¹/₂ tblspn lemon juice

2 medium tomatoes, peeled, seeded and quartered

pinch sugar

3 oranges, segmented

Lemon Cream Dressing

125ml (4fl oz) double cream

2-3 drops lemon juice

salt

1 Separate lettuce leaves and arrange on 4 serving plates.

2 Sprinkle pineapple with most of the lemon juice. Season tomatoes with sugar, pinch salt and leftover lemon juice. Arrange pineapple, tomatoes and orange segments over lettuce.

3 To make dressing, combine cream, remaining lemon juice and a pinch of salt. Spoon a little dressing over fruit and serve remainder separately.

Serves 4

Smoked Trout with Horseradish Cream

2 smoked trout

lemon or lime slices or wedges for garnish

citrus leaves or dill sprigs for garnish

brown bread-and-butter sandwiches to serve

Horseradish Cream

315g (10oz) sour cream

2 tblspn grated fresh horseradish

salt

freshly ground black pepper

1 With a sharp knife, slit trout along back and belly, and cut through skin just behind head and at tail on both sides. Carefully peel off skin and place trout on serving platter or board. Garnish with lemon or lime and citrus leaves or dill.

2 To make cream, mix together sour cream and horseradish with salt and black pepper to taste. To serve, cut through flesh along the back and down the centre; loosen and lift blocks of trout. When the first side is served, turn over and repeat with other side. Serve with cream, black pepper and sandwiches.

Serves 8

Mussel Salad with Celery

2.5kg (5lb) mussels, scrubbed and beards removed

1 onion, sliced

6 parsley sprigs

2-3 crushed black peppercorns

250ml (8fl oz) water

1 small head crisp white celery, finely sliced

lettuce leaves or salad greens to serve, optional

Mustard Sauce

1 tspn dry mustard

1 tblspn lemon juice

185g (6oz) sour cream

salt

freshly ground black pepper

1 Place onion, parsley sprigs, peppercorns and water in a large saucepan and bring to the boil. Add mussels, cover and cook for 5 minutes or until shells open. Discard any unopened mussels. Using a slotted spoon, remove the mussels from liquid. Remove meat from shells and reserve. Discard shells.

2 To make sauce, mix together mustard and lemon juice in a bowl, add sour cream and mix well to combine. Season to taste with salt and black pepper.

3 Place mussels in a bowl, add celery and sauce and toss lightly to coat. Serve salad as is arranged in a lettuce-lined bowl, or a few mussels and salad can be piled in the half-shell before arranging with the greens on the dish.

Serves 4

Clockwise from top: Potato and Watercress Salad, Salad Japonaise, Mussel Salad with Celery

Basque Rice Salad

Smoked Chicken Salad

500g (1lb) smoked chicken, cut into strips

3 red apples, quartered and cored

2 tblspn lemon juice

6 stalks young, crisp celery, sliced

125g (4oz) walnut halves

1 tblspn vegetable oil

2 tspn curry powder

1 small onion, chopped

125g (4oz) mayonnaise

lettuce leaves to serve

1 Place chicken in a bowl. Reserve one apple quarter for garnish. Dice remaining apples, toss with lemon juice and add to chicken wih celery and nuts.

2 Heat oil in a frying pan, add curry powder and onion and cook gently for 5 minutes. Stir onion mixture into mayonnaise, add to salad and toss well. Cover and chill thoroughly.

3 Serve salad piled on crisp lettuce leaves and garnished with reserved sliced apple.

Serves 4

Basque Rice Salad

1/2 tspn saffron threads or pinch of saffron powder

60ml (2fl oz) olive oil

1 bunch spring onions, thinly sliced

440g (14oz) white rice

1 litre (1³/₄pt) chicken stock

1 tspn salt

125g (4oz) salami, cut into strips

500g (1lb) cooked prawns, shelled and deveined

1 red and 1 green pepper, cut into thin strips

4 tblspn chopped fresh parsley

freshly ground black pepper

lemon wedges to serve

1 If using saffron threads, soak in enough warm water to barely cover for 5 minutes.

2 Heat oil in a large saucepan over a medium heat and cook spring onions until just soft. Add rice and stir until grains are well coated with oil. Add stock, salt and soaked or powdered saffron. Stir once, cover tightly and bring to the boil. Reduce heat and barely simmer for 20 minutes or until rice is tender and liquid absorbed.

3 Remove lid and let rice stand a few minutes to let steam escape. Fluff up rice with a fork and turn into a bowl.

4 Add salami, prawns, red and green pepper and parsley to rice, season with salt and black pepper to taste and toss well to combine. Arrange on a large platter. Serve at room temperature with lemon wedges.

Serves 8

Fennel, Onion and Sun-Dried Tomatoes

2 fennel bulbs

6 sun-dried tomatoes in oil

1 red onion, finely sliced

3 tblspn chopped fresh parsley

4 tblspn olive oil

2 tblspn wine vinegar

salt

freshly ground black pepper

1 Wash and trim fennel bulbs and cut lengthwise into thin strips. Cut tomatoes into thin strips, saving any oil for the dressing. Place fennel, tomatoes, onion and parsley in a salad bowl.

2 Place oil from the tomatoes, olive oil and vinegar in a small bowl and whisk to combine, adding salt and black pepper to taste. Pour dressing over salad, cover and let stand for 1 hour. Toss well and serve.

Serves 6

Crunchy Peach Chicken Salad

4 boneless chicken breast fillets

onion slices

parsley sprigs

1 bay leaf

2 peaches, peeled and sliced

125g (4oz) diced celery

4 spring onions, chopped

60g (2oz) chopped pecans

3 tblspn chopped fresh dill

3 tblspn chopped fresh parsley

125g (4oz) mayonnaise

1 tblspn lemon juice

1 tblspn honey

freshly ground black pepper

To garnish

fresh parsley sprigs

1 peach, thinly sliced

tiny lettuce leaves

1 Place chicken in a saucepan with onion slices, parsley sprigs, bay leaf and enough water to barely cover. Bring to simmering, reduce heat and gently poach for 10 minutes or until chicken is just tender. Remove from heat and allow chicken to cool in liquid.

2 Remove skin and bones, slice chicken into long slivers and place in serving bowl. Add peaches, celery, spring onions, pecans, dill and parsley and lightly toss to combine.

3 Place mayonnaise, lemon juice and honey in a small bowl, mix well and season with black pepper to taste. Add to chicken mixture and toss to coat. Arrange salad on four serving plates and garnish with parsley, peach and lettuce.

Serves 6

Fennel, Onion and Sun-Dried Tomatoes

Fresh Peach Muffins

60g (2oz) butter, softened
2 tspn finely grated orange rind
1 large egg
90ml (3fl oz) orange juice
185g (6oz) plain flour
1 tspn baking powder
1 tspn salt
1/2 tspn bicarbonate of soda
170g (5 1/2oz) caster sugar
1 tblspn milk
1 large yellow peach, peeled and chopped or 90g (3oz) canned, drained and diced peaches

1 Preheat oven to 200°C (400°F/ Gas 6). Beat butter and orange rind until light and fluffy, add egg and beat until creamy. Add orange juice and mix well.

2 Sift together flour, baking powder, salt and bicarbonate of soda, add to egg mixture with sugar and quickly mix until just combined, adding milk if mixture is stiff. Fold in peach.

3 Spoon mixture into greased 125ml (4fl oz) capacity muffin tins and bake for 15-20 minutes or until cooked when tested. Turn out and serve warm with butter.

Makes 12

Peaches and Cream

4 large peaches
2 tblspn lemon juice
caster sugar
250g (8oz) double cream, whipped

1 Peel peaches, if liked. Halve and remove stones, then slice and place in a serving bowl.

2 Sprinkle peaches with a little lemon juice and sugar to taste. Lightly toss and serve with cream.

Serves 4

Stewed Stone Fruits and Custard

750g (1 1/2lb) peaches, plums, nectarines and/or apricots
250g (8oz) sugar
250ml (8fl oz) water
1 tspn vanilla essence

Sweet Custard

2 eggs
2 egg yolks
2 tspn cornflour
60g (2oz) sugar
375ml (12fl oz) heated milk

1 Wash and halve fruits and remove stones (or leave whole if preferred). Place sugar and water in a saucepan and bring to simmering, stirring until sugar dissolves. Add fruit and vanilla essence and poach gently until fruit is just tender. Remove pan from heat and set aside to cool. Transfer fruit and syrup to a serving bowl, slipping off skins if liked.

2 To make custard, in top of a double saucepan, lightly beat together whole eggs and egg yolks. Stir in combined cornflour and sugar. Gradually add hot milk, stirring to combine. Place over barely simmering water and cook, stirring constantly, until custard coats the spoon. Remove from heat and cool, stirring occasionally. Serve custard with fruit and syrup.

Serves 6

Fruit Salad with Yogurt Dressing

lettuce leaves
1 large peach, peeled and thickly sliced
1 nectarine, peeled and thickly sliced
1 large banana, peeled and cut into chunks
lemon juice
1 large orange, segmented
2 large scoops cottage or ricotta cheese

Yogurt Dressing

200g (6 1/2oz) natural yogurt
2 tblspn orange juice
1 tblspn honey
2 tspn finely chopped fresh mint
1 tblspn pumpkin seeds or chopped walnuts

1 Arrange 2-4 lettuce leaves on each of 2 salad plates. Sprinkle stone fruits and banana with lemon juice and arrange on lettuce with orange segments and cottage or ricotta cheese.

2 To make dressing, place yogurt, orange juice, honey and mint in a bowl and mix to combine. Spoon dressing over salad and sprinkle with seeds or nuts. Serve with wholemeal toast, if liked.

Serves 2

Fresh Peach Muffins, Peaches and Cream, Stewed Stone Fruits and Custard,

PICNIC PLEASURES

Escape to the great outdoors for a memorable picnic! There is some excellent picnic gear on the market today, including unbreakable plates, mugs and glasses, and insulated bags and boxes to keep food cold, so all these delicious dishes can be easily and safely transported to your favourite picnic spot.

Pissaladiere

250g (8oz) plain flour

1/3 tspn ground cinnamon

90g (3oz) butter, cut into pieces

4-5 tblspn cold water

Pissaladiere Filling

6 tblspn olive oil

1kg (2lb) onions, thinly sliced

3 large cloves garlic, crushed

2 x 440g (14oz) canned tomatoes

1 tspn sugar

2-3 fresh thyme and oregano sprigs or 1/2 teaspoon each dried thyme and oregano

2 tblspn tomato purée

2 x 90g (3oz) canned flat anchovy fillets, drained

8 black olives, halved

1 Place flour and cinnamon into a bowl. Rub in butter until mixture resembles breadcrumbs. Add water and mix to a dough. Knead gently, wrap and chill for 30 minutes.

2 Heat oil in a frying pan, add onion and garlic and cook, stirring, for 20 minutes or until onions are soft, but not brown. Place tomatoes, sugar and herbs in a saucepan and simmer until reduced to 250ml (8fl oz) of pulp. Remove herb sprigs (if using), stir in tomato purée and cooked onion.

3 Preheat oven to 190°C (375°F/ Gas 5). Roll out pastry on a floured surface and line a greased 25cm (10in) flan tin with removable base. Line pastry with baking paper, fill with uncooked rice and bake for 10 minutes.

Remove rice and paper and cook for 5 minutes more.

4 Increase oven to 200°C (400°F/ Gas 6). Spread tomato mixture into pastry case. Halve anchovies lengthwise and arrange in a lattice over filling. Place an olive half in centre of each diamond. Bake for 25 minutes or until cooked and golden. Serve warm.

Serves 8

Spiced Chicken

2kg (4lb) mixed chicken pieces or drum sticks

1 small onion, grated

2 tspn salt

1 tspn freshly ground black pepper

2 tspn crushed garlic

2 tspn chilli paste (sambal oelek) or 1 fresh red chilli, finely chopped

1 tblspn brown sugar

1 tblspn lemon juice

1 tblspn vegetable oil

2 tblspn soy sauce

1 Score skin and flesh of the chicken and place in a shallow dish. Place onion, salt, black pepper, garlic, chilli paste (sambal oelek), sugar, lemon juice, oil and soy sauce in a bowl and mix well. Rub mixture into chicken, cover and let stand 2 hours at room temperature or overnight in the refrigerator.

2 Cook chicken on a rack under a preheated medium grill for 5-8 minutes on each side or until tender. Cool slightly before packing in containers.

Serves 6

Pissaladiere, Spiced Chicken

Artichokes à la Grecque

8 globe artichokes

lemon juice

125ml (4fl oz) olive oil

3 cloves garlic, quartered

2 tomatoes, chopped

2 sprigs each fresh oregano or marjoram

250ml (8fl oz) white wine or chicken stock

chopped fresh parsley for serving

1 Remove tough outside leaves, then cut one-third off the top of each artichoke. Trim the stalk and outer leaves and cut sharp points off each leaf. As each one is prepared, place in a bowl of cold water with some lemon juice to prevent discolouration. Drain on paper towels.

2 Heat oil with garlic in a large, heavy frying pan. Add artichokes, tomatoes, herbs and stock. Cover and simmer gently, turning artichokes frequently, for 45 minutes or until tender. Serve warm or at room temperature sprinkled with parsley.

Serves 8

Kitchen Tip

To eat artichokes, serve with plenty of napkins! Pull off leaves, one at a time, and bite on the base, pulling the leaf between your teeth – for the fleshy morsel at the base. Remove the fuzzy choke and eat the base.

New Potatoes with Dill

1kg (2lb) baby new potatoes

freshly ground black pepper

1 tblspn butter

4 tblspn snipped fresh dill, chives or basil

1 Place potatoes in a saucepan of boiling, salted water. Simmer for 12-15 minutes or until tender and drain.

2 Return potatoes to saucepan with butter and herb of choice and heat through gently.

Serves 8

Aubergine Ratatouille

1kg (2lb) baby aubergine, halved, or 1 large aubergine, cut into finger strips

salt

2 onions, sliced

4 cloves garlic, peeled

1kg (2lb) young green beans, trimmed

4 ripe tomatoes, quartered

freshly ground black pepper

125ml (4fl oz) olive oil

100g (3½oz) black olives

4-5 tblspn chopped fresh parsley

1 Sprinkle aubergine liberally with salt and spread out on a large glass dish. Top with another dish to weigh it down lightly, tip at an angle (put a wooden spoon under one end) and let stand for 30 minutes. Rinse under running water, drain and dry on paper towels.

2 Place onion in a large, heavy saucepan and sprinkle with salt and black pepper. Top with garlic, then beans, aubergine and tomatoes, seasoning each layer. Pour oil evenly over vegetables.

3 Cover pan and bring to simmering. Simmer gently for 40 minutes or until vegetables are tender. Serve garnished with olives and parsley.

Serves 8

Tropical Chicken Salad

125g (4oz) mayonnaise

100g (3½oz) thick natural yogurt

2 tblspn grated, peeled fresh ginger

2 tblspn lime juice

2 tblspn honey

¼ tspn ground cardamom

freshly ground black pepper

4 boneless chicken breast fillets, cooked and cubed

1 mango, chopped, with 2-3 chunks for garnish reserved

½ honeydew melon, cut into cubes

3 tblspn finely chopped fresh mint

pitta bread or flat bread to serve

chicory leaves or other salad greens to serve

1 Place mayonnaise, yogurt, ginger, lime juice, honey and cardamom in a bowl and mix well. Season to taste with salt and black pepper.

2 Add chicken, mango, melon and mint leaves to bowl and toss to coat. Serve salad with bread and greens and garnish with reserved chunks of mango.

Serves 6

Cinnamon Picnic Cake

315g (10oz) sugar

60g (2oz) chopped mixed nuts

2 tspn ground cinnamon

125g (4oz) butter

2 eggs

1 tspn vanilla essence

1 tblspn lemon juice

250g (8oz) plain flour

½ tspn baking powder

½ tspn bicarbonate of soda

¼ tspn salt

250g (8oz) sour cream

1 Preheat oven to 180°C (350°F/ Gas 4). Combine 60g (2oz) sugar with the nuts and cinnamon and set aside. Beat butter and remaining sugar until light and fluffy. Add eggs, vanilla essence and lemon juice and beat well until creamy.

2 Sift flour with baking powder, bicarbonate of soda and salt, and add alternately with sour cream to the butter mixture.

3 Pour batter into a greased and lined 23cm (9in) square cake tin and sprinkle with cinnamon mixture. Bake for 35-40 minutes or until a skewer inserted in centre comes out clean. Cool completely.

Serves 8

Anticlockwise from top: New Potatoes with Dill, Artichokes à la Grecque, Korean Beef Salad, Tropical Chicken Salad, Aubergine Ratatouille

Korean Beef Salad

6 tblspn sake or dry sherry

6 tblspn soy sauce

3 tblspn sesame oil

1¹/₂ tspn coarsely ground black pepper

750g (1¹/₂lb) boneless sirloin or rump steak, trimmed

4 onions, chopped

Korean Salad Dressing

1 clove garlic, chopped

1 tblspn Dijon mustard

2 tspn honey

3 tblspn rice vinegar

3 tblspn soy sauce

3 tblspn sesame oil

8 tblspn vegetable oil

250g (8oz) button mushrooms, halved

125g (4oz) mangetout, blanched and drained

pitta bread to serve

90g (3oz) alfalfa or mangetout sprouts for garnish

1 In a large shallow glass dish, place sake or sherry, soy sauce, 3 tablespoons sesame oil and black pepper and mix well. Add steak and onions, cover and let marinate for at least 3 hours at room temperature, or in refrigerator overnight. Stir and turn steak several times.

2 Place garlic, mustard, honey, vinegar and soy sauce in a large bowl and whisk constantly, gradually adding sesame oil and 6 tablespoons vegetable oil, until mixture thickens (dressing may be prepared a day in advance and kept covered and chilled).

3 Remove beef and onions from marinade. Pat steak very dry and reserve half the marinade. Heat remaining vegetable oil in a large, heavy frying pan over a medium-high heat. Add steak and cook, turning once, for 4-5 minutes on each side for medium-rare. Transfer steak to a cutting board allow to stand for 10 minutes.

4 Add onions to same pan and cook, stirring, for 5 minutes or until tender. Using a slotted spoon, transfer onions to bowl containing dressing. Add mushrooms with reserved marinade to pan and cook until almost all liquid evaporates. Add mushrooms to dressing with mangetout.

5 Slice beef thinly across the grain, add to vegetable mixture and toss well. Serve salad with pitta bread, garnished with sprouts.

Serves 8

Peperonata

2 tblspn olive oil

45g (1¹/₂oz) butter

2 large onions, chopped

6 red peppers, cut into strips

2 cloves garlic, crushed

salt

freshly ground black pepper

6 ripe tomatoes, peeled and quartered

2 tblspn fresh basil or oregano leaves

1 Heat oil and butter in a heavy frying pan over a medium heat. Add onions and cook, stirring, until soft and golden. Add red peppers and garlic to pan, season to taste with salt and black pepper, cover and simmer for 15 minutes.

2 Add tomatoes to pan, stir well and cook gently, uncovered, for 30 minutes or until peppers are tender and mixture thickened. Add basil or oregano just before serving as a relish or part of an antipasto tray.

Serves 6

Marinated Mushrooms

1kg (2lb) firm white button mushrooms

500ml (16fl oz) wine vinegar

185ml (6fl oz) olive oil

3 cloves garlic, crushed

¹/₂ bay leaf

fresh thyme sprig

6-8 each whole peppercorns and coriander seeds

1 Wipe over mushrooms and cook in boiling salted water for 4 minutes, drain and dry. Place mushrooms in clean preserving or jam jars.

2 Place vinegar, oil, garlic, bay leaf and thyme in a saucepan, bring to the boil, then pour over mushrooms. Cover and allow to marinate for at least 4-5 days. Serve as an appetiser with crusty bread.

Serves 8

Rabbit Pistachio Terrine

750g (1¹/₂lb) boneless rabbit meat, minced

500g (1lb) minced sausage meat

500g (1lb) belly pork, trimmed and minced or finely chopped

155g (5oz) breadcrumbs, made from stale bread

1 small onion, finely chopped

1 clove garlic, crushed

¹/₂ tspn dried thyme

2 tblspn Pernod

1 tblspn salt

¹/₄ tspn freshly ground black pepper

1 egg, beaten

125g (4oz) chopped pistachio nuts or walnuts

250g (8oz) streaky bacon rashers, rind removed

1 Preheat oven to 180°C (350°F/ Gas 4). Place rabbit mince in a large bowl with sausage mince, pork and breadcrumbs. Add onion, garlic, thyme, Pernod, salt, black pepper, egg, and nuts and mix thoroughly with a wooden spoon.

2 Line a 2.5 litre (4pt) terrine or loaf tin with bacon. Spoon rabbit mixture into tin and level the surface. Cut remaining bacon into thin strips and arrange on top of mixture in a lattice design. Cover tightly with foil or lid and bake for 1¹/₂ hours.

3 Remove from oven, remove lid and place a weight on top of terrine. Let stand until cool, then refrigerate overnight. Serve sliced with crusty bread.

Serves 10-12

Clockwise from top: Peperonata, Marinated Mushrooms, Rabbit Pistachio Terrine, Devilled Cutlets

Devilled Cutlets

8 lamb cutlets

1 tspn each salt, dry mustard, ground ginger and curry powder

2 tspn sugar

2 tblspn each tomato relish and fruit chutney

1 tblspn Worcestershire sauce

1 Trim cutlets and rub well with mixed spices and sugar. Allow to stand at room temperature to marinate for 1 hour.

2 Cook cutlets under a preheated medium grill for 3 minutes on each side. Place relish, chutney and Worcestershire sauce in a bowl, mix well and spread over cutlets. Cook for 2 minutes more or until cooked to your liking.

3 Cool cutlets and package for picnic with paper napkins.

Serves 4

Parsleyed Tongue Mould

1 x 500g (1lb) ox tongue, corned or fresh

6 whole cloves

1 bouquet garni

1 onion, sliced

1 carrot, sliced

1 stalk celery, sliced

1/2 tspn salt

500g (1lb) ham steaks or thickly sliced leg ham, cubed

250ml (8fl oz) chicken stock

250ml (8fl oz) dry white wine

freshly ground black pepper and nutmeg

45g (1 1/2oz) finely chopped fresh parsley

2 tblspn gelatine

1-2 tblspn wine vinegar

1 Place tongue in a saucepan with water to cover, add cloves, bouquet garni, onion, carrot, celery and salt. Bring slowly to the boil, skim the surface, cover and

simmer for 2-3 hours or until tongue is tender. Remove from heat and allow tongue to cool in liquid.

2 Remove any bones and fat from tongue. Slit underside of skin and carefully peel off. Cut tongue lengthwise into thick slices, then into small cubes.

3 Place tongue and ham cubes in saucepan, add stock and wine and season to taste with black pepper and nutmeg. Bring to simmering and simmer for 15 minutes. Drain cubes, reserving liquid.

4 Arrange cubes in a 1.25-1.5 litre (2-2 1/2pt) loaf tin or bowl which has been rinsed out with water and lightly dusted with some of the parsley.

5 Soften gelatine in a little water and stir into reserved hot liquid until dissolved. Add remaining parsley and vinegar. Cool until mixture is syrupy, then pour over cubes in mould.

6 Chill until set, at least 4 hours or overnight. Unmould and cut into thick slices. Serve, if liked, with a little malt vinegar and mustard of choice.

Serves 8

Italian Salmon Salad

250g (8oz) pasta shells

440g (14oz) canned salmon, drained and flaked

1 red pepper, diced

1 cucumber, finely diced

3 hard-boiled eggs, quartered

10 black olives, halved

185ml (6fl oz) vinaigrette dressing

2 tomatoes, quartered

1 Cook pasta in boiling water following package directions until tender, drain thoroughly and set aside to cool.

2 Place salmon in a bowl and flake with a fork. Add red pepper, cucumber, eggs, olives and pasta and lightly mix to combine. Reserve 1 tablespoon dressing. Pour remaining dressing over pasta mixture and toss lightly.

3 Serve salad with tomatoes and drizzled with reserved dressing.

Serves 6

Prawn and White Bean Salad

3 x 315g (10oz) canned cannellini beans, rinsed and drained

185g (6oz) celery, thinly sliced

1 small red onion, thinly sliced

6 tblspn olive oil

3 cloves garlic, chopped

1/2 tspn dried hot red pepper flakes

750g (1 1/2lb) prawns, shelled and deveined

60ml (2fl oz) lemon juice, or to taste

3 tblspn chopped fresh parsley

1 tblspn finely chopped fresh oregano or 1 tspn dried oregano

8 lettuce leaves

1 Place drained beans, celery and onion in a bowl and lightly mix to combine. Heat half the oil in a large heavy frying pan and cook garlic and red pepper flakes for 30 seconds or until fragrant. Add prawns and cook, stirring, for 2-3 minutes or until just tender.

2 Add prawn mixture to beans with lemon juice, remaining oil, herbs, salt and black pepper to taste and toss well. Cover and chill until served.

3 At the picnic, arrange 2 lettuce leaves on each plate and top with salad.

Serves 4

Parsleyed Tongue Mould

Olive Herb Bread

2 large eggs

75g (2¹/₂oz) pitted black olives, chopped

2 tblspn olive oil

2 tblspn chopped fresh parsley

1 tspn chopped fresh rosemary or oregano

125ml (4fl oz) milk

250g (8oz) plain flour

1 tblspn sugar

2 tspn baking powder

¹/₄ tspn salt

1 Preheat oven to 180°C (350°F/ Gas 4). Beat eggs until frothy and stir in olives, oil, herbs and milk. Sift flour, sugar, baking powder and salt into egg mixture and quickly mix to make a soft dough.

2 With floured hands, knead dough gently and shape into a domed round on a greased baking sheet. Bake for 1 hour or until loaf sounds hollow when tapped. Cool on a wire rack.

Makes 1 loaf

Tortellini Salad

500g (1lb) frozen tortellini or other filled pasta

6 sun-dried tomatoes, sliced

3 stalks celery, sliced

8-10 black olives

3 tblspn chopped fresh parsley

1 tblspn chopped fresh basil

250g (8oz) cherry tomatoes, washed

Vinaigrette Dressing

2 tspn French mustard

1 tblspn tarragon vinegar

6 tblspn olive oil

1 tspn salt

freshly ground black pepper

1 Cook tortellini in boiling, salted water following package directions until *al dente*. Drain well.

2 To make dressing, place mustard, vinegar, oil, salt and black pepper to taste in a large bowl and whisk until well combined. Add hot pasta, toss to coat and set aside to cool.

3 Add tomatoes, celery and olives to pasta, mix well and transfer to serving bowl. Top with parsley, basil and tomatoes. Toss lightly before servng.

Serves 6

Pâté de Campagne

1kg (2lb) minced pork and veal

500g (1lb) fresh pork fat, minced or finely chopped

1 tblspn salt

1 tspn freshly ground black pepper

2 tspn chopped fresh thyme

2 tspn chopped fresh oregano

1 tspn ground allspice

1 tspn dried tarragon

4 garlic cloves, chopped

125ml (4fl oz) cognac or brandy

60ml (2fl oz) dry vermouth or sherry

4 eggs, lightly beaten

1 onion, finely chopped, sautéed in butter until soft and drained

220g (7oz) chicken livers, trimmed and quartered

90g (3oz) fresh walnut pieces

6 thinly sliced bacon rashers, rind removed

2 bay leaves

3 whole juniper berries

1 Place pork and veal mince in a large bowl with pork fat, salt, pepper, thyme, oregano, allspice, tarragon, garlic, cognac, vermouth, eggs and sautéed onion. Mix thoroughly without overworking the mixture, then lightly fold in livers and walnuts.

2 Preheat oven to 180°C (350°F/ Gas 4). Line base and sides of a 23 x 10 x 9cm (9 x 4 x 3¹/₂in) loaf tin with bacon, allowing ends to hang over the sides. Pack meat mixture into tin, pressing out air pockets and slightly mounding the centre. Top with bay leaves and juniper berries.

3 Fold bacon ends over meat, then cover with aluminium foil, pressing snugly to seal. Place tin in a larger tin or deep baking dish filled with enough boiling water to come halfway up sides of the tin. Bake for 2¹/₂ hours.

4 Remove tin from water, top with a plate, then a heavy weight and set aside to cool for several hours. Remove weight and plate and refrigerate until cold.

5 Remove pâté from loaf tin, scrape surfaces clean and return to clean tin. Refrigerate at least 2 days before serving to allow flavours to mellow. Serve sliced at room temperature.

Serves 10

Mixed Vegetable Salad

500g (1lb) frozen broad beans, cooked

2 small carrots, diced and cooked

90g (3oz) thinly sliced celery

1 each red and green pepper, chopped

6-8 spring onions, finely chopped

440g (14oz) canned sweet corn kernels, drained

375g (12oz) canned red kidney beans, rinsed and drained

1 x quantity Vinaigrette Dressing, see Tortellini Salad this page

45g (1¹/₂oz) chopped fresh parsley

3 tblspn chopped fresh mint or basil

1 Place broad beans, carrots, celery, red and green pepper, spring onions, corn and kidney beans in a large bowl.

2 Prepare vinaigrette, pour over salad and mix well. Set aside to marinate at least 30 minutes at room temperature, or several hours in the refrigerator. Sprinkle with herbs and toss before serving.

Serves 10

Clockwise from top: Olive Herb Bread, Tortellini Salad, Pâté de Campagne, Mixed Vegetable Salad

Courgette Nut Bread

3 eggs

500g (1lb) sugar

3 tspn vanilla essence

250ml (8fl oz) safflower or light olive oil

350g (11oz) courgettes, unpeeled and grated

125g (4oz) plain flour

125g (4oz) wholemeal flour

1/4 tspn baking powder

1 tspn salt

1 tspn bicarbonate of soda

3 tspn ground cinnamon

125g (4oz) chopped walnuts

1 Preheat oven to 180°C (350°F/ Gas 4). Grease and line the base and two long sides of two 23cm (9in) loaf tins with greaseproof paper.

2 Beat eggs in a large bowl until light and foamy. Gradually add sugar, then vanilla essence and oil, beating constantly until mixture is thick and mousse-like. Stir in courgettes. Sift together flours with baking powder, salt, bicarbonate of soda and cinnamon and fold into batter with the walnuts.

3 Pour batter into tins and bake for 1-1¼ hours or until cooked when tested with a skewer. Cool briefly in tins, then turn out and cool on wire racks.

Makes 2 loaves

Courgette and Pepper Frittata

2 tblspn olive oil

1 small onion, finely chopped

250g (8oz) courgettes, thinly sliced

1/2 red pepper, finely chopped

1/2 green pepper, finely chopped

salt

freshly ground black pepper

8 large eggs

90g (3oz) grated Parmesan cheese

2 tblspn chopped fresh parsley

1 Heat half the oil in a 23cm (9in) frying pan and cook onion, courgettes and red and green peppers over a medium heat, stirring constantly for 10 minutes or until tender. Season to taste with salt and black pepper.

2 Place eggs, half the Parmesan cheese and parsley in a bowl and whisk to combine. Stir in vegetable mixture.

3 In same pan, heat remaining oil until hot, but not smoking. Add egg mixture, distributing vegetables evenly, and cook without stirring, for 4-5 minutes, or until edge is set but centre is still soft. Sprinkle with remaining Parmesan cheese.

4 If necessary, protect frying pan handle with a double thickness of foil. Place pan under a preheated medium grill and cook frittata for 2-3 minutes or until cheese is golden. Let cool in pan for 5 minutes, then run a knife around the edge and slide frittata onto a serving plate. Serve at room temperature cut into wedges.

Serves 6

Chicken Tourtiere

1 x quantity Rich Shortcrust Pastry, see recipe this page

140g (4½oz) short-grain rice

375ml (12fl oz) water

750g (1½lb) chicken thighs and legs, boned and skinned

500g (1lb) boneless chicken breast fillets

1 bunch spring onions, finely chopped

2 tspn grated lemon rind

2 tblspn lemon juice

1 egg, beaten

salt

freshly ground black pepper

4 hard-boiled eggs

beaten egg for glazing

1 To make filling, cook rice in water in covered saucepan over low heat until rice is tender and all liquid is absorbed.

2 Reserve 3 chicken breasts and cut remaining chicken into cubes. Place cubes, in batches, in a food processor and process until minced.

3 Preheat oven to 180°C (350°F/ Gas 4). Place chicken mince in a large bowl, add rice, spring onions, lemon rind, lemon juice, 1 beaten egg, salt and black pepper to taste and mix well to combine.

4 Roll out three-quarters of the pastry to line a deep loaf tin (or use a flan tin or springform with a removable base), allowing pastry to slightly overhang rim. Half-fill tin with rice mixture. Cut reserved chicken into long thick strips and place half the strips lengthwise on top of rice. Arrange hard-boiled eggs down centre. Top with remaining chicken strips, then remaining rice mixture.

5 Roll out remaining pastry to cover filling, trim edges and crump together to seal. Make a small cut in the centre and decorate, if liked, with pastry scraps. Brush with egg glaze and bake for 1-1½ hours or until filling is cooked and pastry well-browned. Cool to room temperature, then refrigerate until cold before removing from mould and slicing.

Serves 10

Rich Shortcrust Pastry

375g (12oz) plain flour

250g (8oz) unsalted butter

1 egg yolk mixed with 1½ tblspn water

1 Sift flour into a large bowl. Cut butter into small pieces and rub into flour with fingertips until mixture resembles coarse breadcrumbs.

2 Make a well in centre of the flour mixture, add combined egg yolk and water and lightly mix to make a firm dough. Knead dough on a lightly floured surface until smooth. Wrap in plastic food wrap and chill for 20-30 minutes.

Chicken Tourtiere

THE LONG SUMMER LUNCH

Welcome summer by entertaining family and friends with lazy lunches 'al fresco'. Many of the dishes can be prepared in advance and just need a few minutes to assemble before serving, which leaves you free to spend more time with your guests.

Poached Salmon

750ml (1¼pt) water or half white wine, half water

1 tblspn vinegar (omit if wine is used)

1 onion, sliced

5-6 parsley sprigs

1 thyme sprig

1 bay leaf

6 peppercorns

1 tspn salt

1.5kg (3lb) fresh centre-cut salmon or ocean trout

1 cucumber, thinly sliced

mango slices and salad greens to serve

Mango Mint Sauce

1 mango

375ml (12fl oz) light olive oil

125ml (4fl oz) balsamic vinegar or red wine vinegar

8 fresh mint leaves, shredded

1 Preheat oven to 160°C (325°F/ Gas 3). Bring water, vinegar, onion, parsley, thyme, bay leaf, peppercorns and salt to the boil, then simmer for 10 minutes. Pour into a non-metallic baking dish large enough to hold fish.

2 Place fish on a rack in the dish, cover with foil and bake, basting every 15 minutes, for 30-35 minutes or until just tender.

3 To make sauce, cut flesh from mango, place in a food processor and process, gradually adding oil, then vinegar and mint leaves, until smooth and thick.

4 Carefully lift fish from liquid and remove skin. Place fish on a serving dish, decorate with cucumber slices and serve with mango slices, salad greens and sauce.

Serves 8

Avocado Julienne Salad

1 red or green pepper

1 carrot

4 spring onions

2 avocados, halved and stoned

Mustard Dressing

2 tblspn olive oil

1 tblspn each wine vinegar and balsamic vinegar

2 tspn rum, optional

1 tspn French mustard

freshly ground black pepper

dash Tabasco sauce

1 Cut red or green pepper, carrot and spring onions into fine julienne strips. Blanch strips in boiling water for a few seconds, drain, rinse and pat dry with paper towels and place in a bowl.

2 To make dressing, place oil, vinegars, rum (if using) and mustard in a screwtop jar with black pepper and Tabasco sauce to taste and shake well to combine. Pour over vegetables and toss.

3 To serve, pile vegetables into avocado halves.

Serves 4

Clockwise from top: Tropical Fruit Fondue (page 36), Poached Salmon with Mango Mint Sauce, Avocado Julienne Salad,

Tropical Fruit Fondue

2-3 each kiwi fruit and tamarillos, passionfruit or star fruit, sliced (other fruits such as grapes, strawberries, figs and mangoes may be used)

Fondue Sauce

250g (8oz) sour cream

1 tblspn sieved apricot jam

2 tspn finely chopped fresh ginger

2 tblspn desiccated coconut

1 To make sauce, place all ingredients in a bowl and mix to combine. Chill thoroughly.

2 Prepare fruit and arrange on a platter. If liked, simply halve kiwi fruit, tamarillos and passionfruit. Spoon sauce over fruit or place in small dishes and use as a dip.

Serves 6

Chicken Tonnato

600ml (1pt) chicken stock

1 stalk celery, sliced

1 onion, quartered

2 fresh parsley sprigs

1 bay leaf

few black peppercorns

6 boneless chicken breast fillets

lemon wedges, whole capers and chopped fresh parsley for garnish

Tuna Sauce

220g (7oz) canned tuna in oil

5 anchovy fillets

3 tblspn lemon juice

3 tblspn capers

375ml (12fl oz) olive oil

315g (10oz) mayonnaise

freshly ground black pepper

1 Place stock, celery, onion, parsley sprigs, bay leaf and peppercorns in a large saucepan. Bring to the boil and boil for 3-5 minutes. Add fillets, reduce heat, cover and gently poach for 6-8 minutes or until chicken is just tender. Remove from heat and set aside to cool in liquid.

2 To make sauce, place undrained tuna, anchovies, lemon juice and capers in a blender or food processor and process, gradually adding oil, until mixture is creamy. Transfer mixture to a bowl, add mayonnaise and mix until combined. Season to taste with black pepper.

3 Remove chicken from liquid and cut into thick slices or chunks. Arrange a layer of chicken on serving dish and spread with sauce to thickly coat. Top with more chicken and sauce, repeating layers until chicken is used. Reserve 125ml (4oz) sauce for garnish. Cover and marinate for 2 hours at room temperature or refrigerate overnight.

4 Stir reserved sauce and spread over chicken. Garnish with lemon wedges, capers and parsley and bring to room temperature before serving.

Serves 8

Vegetables à la Grecque

6-8 small courgettes

250g (8oz) button mushrooms

6-8 mature spring onions

250g (8oz) green beans

1 red pepper

750ml (1¼pt) water

185ml (6fl oz) olive oil

3 tomatoes, peeled and seeded

2 cloves garlic, crushed

3 tblspn finely chopped fresh parsley

3 tblspn lemon juice

2 tspn dried tarragon

½ tspn dried thyme

1 bay leaf

salt

freshly ground black pepper

1 Trim courgettes and cut into thick diagonal slices or halve lengthwise. Trim mushroom stalks. Trim spring onions, leaving a little of the green tops. Top and tail beans, cut red pepper into thick strips.

2 Place water, oil, tomatoes, garlic, parsley, lemon juice and herbs in a heavy saucepan or flameproof casserole, cover and bring to the boil. Reduce heat, add courgettes and cook for 6-8 minutes or until tender but firm. Using a slotted spoon, remove courgettes and place in a ceramic or glass serving dish.

3 Cook remaining vegetables separately in the oil mixture: mushrooms 4-5 minutes, spring onions 8-10 minutes, beans 5 minutes, and red pepper 3 minutes — adding each to the courgettes. Vegetables should be soft but still crisp. When all vegetables are cooked, season cooking liquid with salt and black pepper to taste and pour over vegetables. Let mixture cool, then cover and chill until served.

Serves 6

Lettuce and Watercress Salad

3 heads lettuce such as butterhead, radicchio, curly endive, mignonette or mixture

1 small bunch watercress

½ bunch radishes, sliced

2-3 tblspn extra virgin olive oil

2 tspn lemon juice

salt

freshly ground black pepper

1 Rinse and dry lettuce and watercress and remove any coarse stems. Wrap loosely in a clean tea-towel, place in a plastic bag and chill until crisp.

2 In a salad bowl, toss together lettuce, watercress and radishes. Drizzle with olive oil, lemon juice and salt and black pepper to taste. Toss salad until well combined.

Serves 6-8

Clockwise from top: Lettuce and Watercress Salad, Vegetables à la Grecque, Chicken Tonnato

Grilled Quail with Wild Rice Pilau

6 quail

1 tspn rosemary

freshly ground black pepper

1 tblspn olive oil

170g (5¹/₂oz) wild rice

170g (5¹/₂oz) long-grain rice

750ml (1¹/₄pt) water

1 tblspn butter

1 tspn salt

60ml (2fl oz) olive oil

30g (1oz) pine nuts

2 tblspn currants

1 Split each quail down the backbone, spread out and flatten breast with the broad side of a meat cleaver. Season with rosemary and black pepper to taste. Brush with 1 tablespoon olive oil. Place on a plate and allow to marinate for 30 minutes at room temperature.

2 Place rices, water, butter and salt in a heavy saucepan. Bring to the boil, stir and cover with lid. Reduce heat and simmer gently for 20 minutes. Remove lid, fluff up with a fork.

3 Heat 60ml (2fl oz) oil in a frying pan, add pine nuts and currants and cook, stirring, for 5 minutes or until golden. Toss through rice.

4 Cook quail under a preheated medium grill for 3-4 minutes on each side or until cooked to your liking. To serve, pile rice on a heated platter and arrange quail on top.

Serves 6

Fresh Fruit with Mascarpone

1 mango

2 peaches

2 nectarines

250g (8oz) cherries

250g (8oz) fresh raspberries or blueberries

3 tblspn orange juice

2 tblspn liqueur of your choice, optional

250g (8oz) mascarpone or sour cream

1 tblspn soft brown sugar

1 Slice stone fruits, place in a bowl with cherries and berries. Sprinkle over the orange juice and the liqueur (if using). Cover with plastic food wrap and refrigerate, stirring occasionally, for several hours to allow flavours to mellow.

2 Place mascarpone or sour cream in a bowl, add sugar and mix to combine.

3 Serve fruit on flat dessert plates with mascarpone and accompany with crisp sweet biscuits, if liked.

Serves 6

Grilled Quail with Wild Rice Pilau,
Fresh Fruit with Mascarpone

Roast Chicken Fantasia

2 x 1.5kg (3lb) chickens

salt

2 bacon rashers, halved

6 fresh sage leaves

4 fresh rosemary sprigs

2 tblspn each butter and oil

12 thin slices prosciutto or ham

2 brown paper bags, each large enough to contain 1 chicken, or large sheets of baking paper

1 Remove excess fat from chickens. Season cavities with salt to taste, then fill each with half the bacon, sage and rosemary. Truss chickens into neat shapes with string.

2 Heat half the butter and oil in a frying pan over moderately high heat and quickly brown 1 chicken on all sides. Repeat with other chicken. Remove from pan, cool slightly and then drape each chicken with prosciutto or ham.

3 Preheat oven to 180°C (350°F/ Gas 4). Place each bird in a bag, brush bags with oil and tie securely closed with string. If using baking paper, fold loosely around chicken, folding edges to make a seal. Place the bags in an oiled baking dish and bake for 15 minutes. Pierce bags once or twice with a sharp knife and continue cooking for 1 hour longer.

4 Remove from oven and cut away bags, allowing juices to drain onto a heated serving platter. Line the platter with prosciutto or ham and arrange the chicken on top, whole or jointed. Serve with new potatoes.

Serves 6-8

Roast Leg of Lamb with Watercress

2kg (4lb) leg of lamb

2 cloves garlic, slivered

salt

freshly ground black pepper

1 tblspn olive oil

125g (4oz) breadcrumbs, made from stale bread

4 tblspn chopped fresh parsley

250ml (8fl oz) dry white wine

1 bunch watercress, washed and trimmed

lemon wedges to serve

1 Preheat oven to 220°C (425°F/ Gas 7). Trim excess fat from lamb, cut small slits with sharp knife and insert slivers of garlic. Rub lamb with salt and black pepper to taste and brush with oil. Place lamb in a roasting tin and cook for 10 minutes. Reduce oven temperature to 180°C (350°F/Gas 4) and continue cooking for 1 hour.

2 Remove lamb from oven. Combine the breadcrumbs and parsley with a little of the lamb juices and press mixture onto lamb to coat. Cook for 10 minutes longer or until crumbs are toasted. Transfer to a heated serving platter, cover and allow to rest for 10 minutes before carving.

3 Pour off fat from tin, add wine to meat juices and bring to the boil over high heat, scraping bottom and sides of tin until liquid reduces by half.

4 To serve, place watercress around and under the lamb, reserving a sprig for each plate. Carve lamb into neat slices, spoon a little of the sauce and crumbs over the slices. Serve with wedges of lemon.

Serves 6-8

Beef Fillet with Herbs

1.25kg (2lb8oz) beef fillet, in 1 piece

30g (1oz) butter

125ml (4fl oz) Madeira or port

salt

freshly ground black pepper

4 anchovies, chopped or 1 tblspn capers

4 tblspn chopped mixed fresh herbs

salad greens such as lettuce, rocket, watercress

cherry tomatoes, halved

1 Preheat oven to 200°C (400°F/ Gas 6). Trim fillet and tie into a neat shape. Heat butter in a heavy roasting tin or iron casserole over high heat and quickly brown fillet on all sides. Pour half the wine over beef and sprinkle with salt and black pepper to taste.

2 Place meat in oven and roast, basting frequently, for 25 minutes. Remove from oven and allow to rest for 10 minutes. Stir remaining wine into roasting tin, bring quickly to the boil and spoon over meat. Combine anchovies and herbs and press onto meat.

3 Tear greens into bite-sized pieces and arrange on platter with tomatoes. Slice meat and arrange on salad.

Serves 6

Onion Rosemary Bread

90g (3oz) unsalted butter

1 large onion, finely chopped

1¹/₂ tblspn roughly chopped fresh rosemary

2 x 7g (¹/₄oz) sachets active dried yeast

1 tspn sugar

500ml (16fl oz) warm water

2 tspn salt

820-875g (1lb10oz-1lb12oz) plain flour

vegetable oil for glazing

1 Melt butter in a saucepan over a medium heat and cook onion, stirring, until soft. Add rosemary and cook for 1 minute. Cool.

2 Place yeast, sugar and water in a mixing bowl and let stand for 10 minutes or until foamy. Stir in onion mixture, salt and 625g (1lb4oz) of the flour until combined. Stir in enough of the remaining flour to make a soft, not sticky dough.

3 Turn dough onto a floured surface and knead for 6-8 minutes or until smooth and elastic. Place in an oiled bowl, turning dough to coat, cover with plastic food wrap and let rise in a warm place for 1-1¹/₂ hours or until doubled.

4 Punch dough down and shape into a ball. Halve dough and roll each half on a lightly oiled surface to a 30 x 23cm (12 x 9in) rectangle. Roll up from a short end Swiss roll fashion and pinch seams to seal. Place each roll in a greased 23 x 12 x 8cm (9 x 5 x 3in) loaf tin.

5 Brush lightly with oil, make deep diagonal slashes in top of each, cover loosely with a tea-towel and let rise in a warm place for 45 minutes or until loaves rise to tops of tins.

6 Preheat oven to 200°C (400F/ Gas 6). Bake loaves for 35-45 minutes or until golden and sound hollow when tapped. Turn loaves out onto a wire rack and cool completely.

Makes 2 loaves

Salad Contadina

500g (1lb) new potatoes, cooked and sliced

500g (1lb) green beans, cooked

315g (10oz) canned cannellini beans, rinsed and drained

3 tomatoes, quartered

1 red onion, sliced and separated into rings

2 tblspn chopped fresh basil

Vinaigrette Dressing

125ml (4fl oz) olive oil

2 tblspn wine vinegar

1 tspn Dijon mustard

1 clove garlic, crushed

salt

freshly ground black pepper

1 To make dressing, place oil, vinegar, mustard, garlic and salt and black pepper to taste in a screwtop jar and shake well to combine.

2 Place potatoes, green beans and cannellini beans in a salad bowl, add dressing and toss well to coat. Decorate salad with a ring of tomatoes and onions and sprinkle with basil.

Serves 6

Escabeche of Tongue

1 large (or 2 small) ox tongue

water

6 whole allspice

6 whole cloves

6 black peppercorns

1 onion, sliced

1 bouquet garni

1 carrot, quartered

1 stalk celery, cut into pieces

Egg Sauce

4 cloves garlic, chopped

6 tblspn olive oil

3 tblspn wine vinegar

dash Tabasco sauce

45g (1¹/₂oz) finely chopped fresh parsley

2 hard-boiled eggs, finely chopped

salt

freshly ground black pepper

1 Rinse tongue, curl it into a deep saucepan and cover with cold water. Add allspice, cloves, black peppercorns, onion, bouquet garni, carrot and celery to pan and bring to the boil. Reduce heat to low, cover and simmer for 2-3 hours or until tongue is tender when tested at the root end with a skewer.

2 Allow tongue to cool for 1 hour in the liquid, then lift out, remove root and any bones and peel off skin. Place on a flat plate, cover with plastic food wrap and chill until needed.

3 To make sauce, place garlic and olive oil in a bowl and beat in the vinegar and Tabasco sauce until mixture is thick and creamy. Stir in parsley and eggs and season to taste with salt and black pepper.

4 Slice tongue and place in a serving bowl. Spoon sauce over and toss lightly to coat. Cover with plastic food wrap and chill overnight before serving.

Serves 8

Clockwise from top: Chocolate Caramel Pecan Tarts, Onion Rosemary Bread, Escabeche of Tongue, Salad Contadina

Chocolate Caramel Pecan Tarts

125g (4oz) dark chocolate, roughly chopped

315g (10oz) pecans, roughly chopped and toasted

Chocolate Filling

185g (6oz) sugar

500g (1lb) light corn or golden syrup

3 tblspn unsalted butter

4 large eggs

1/2 tspn vanilla essence

grated chocolate to decorate

Shortcrust Pastry

315g (10oz) plain flour

90g (3oz) cold unsalted butter, roughly chopped

1/4 tspn salt

4 tblspn iced water

1 egg, beaten

1 To make pastry, place flour, butter and salt in a food processor and process until mixture resembles breadcrumbs. With machine running, add water and egg and process just until dough forms a ball. Halve dough, shape into flat rounds, wrap and chill for 1 hour.

2 Roll out dough on a lightly floured surface to fit 2 x 23cm (9in) tart tins with removable bases. Melt chocolate over simmering water, stirring until smooth. Brush over pastry cases and chill for 15 minutes. Divide nuts between cases.

3 Preheat oven to 190°C (375°F/ Gas 5). In a heavy saucepan, heat sugar over a medium-high heat, stirring constantly, until melted and a deep caramel colour. Remove from heat, carefully stir in corn or golden syrup, return to heat and cook, stirring, until smooth. Stir in butter and remove from heat.

4 Place eggs and vanilla essence in a bowl and whisk constantly, adding caramel in a slow stream, until blended. Divide filling between cases, coating the nuts completely.

5 Place tarts on a baking sheet and bake for 35-40 minutes or until pastry is pale golden. Cool on wire racks. Sprinkle with grated chocolate before serving.

Serves 12

Mediterranean-Style Stuffed Peppers

8 red or green peppers

1 1/2 tspn salt

2 tblspn olive oil

125ml (4fl oz) boiling water

Rice Stuffing

170g (5 1/2oz) rice

60ml (2fl oz) olive oil

2 onions, finely chopped

2 tblspn pine nuts

1 tspn salt

250g (8oz) undrained canned tomatoes

125ml (4fl oz) boiling water

45g (1 1/2oz) currants or chopped raisins

1/4 tspn ground allspice

1/4 tspn freshly ground black pepper

2 tspn sugar

2 tblspn chopped fresh mint

1 To make stuffing, place rice in a bowl pour over boiling water to cover and let stand until water cools. Drain, rinse with cold water and drain again.

2 Heat oil in a saucepan, add onions, pine nuts and salt and cook, stirring, until onions are golden. Add rice and stir until well coated with oil. Add tomatoes, boiling water, currants or raisins, allspice, black pepper, sugar and mint. Reduce heat, cover and cook for 15 minutes or until liquid is absorbed. Cool completely.

3 Cut tops off peppers and remove seeds. Loosely fill with stuffing. Arrange, close together, in a heavy saucepan and sprinkle with salt and olive oil. Pour over boiling water, cover and simmer for 25-30 minutes or until tender. Add more water, if necessary, to avoid burning. Cool in saucepan, then refrigerate until served.

Serves 8

Apple and Cherry Strudel

100g (3 1/2oz) caster sugar

1 1/2 tspn ground cinnamon

60g (2oz) coarsely chopped walnuts

4 large cooking apples, peeled and thinly sliced

2 tblspn lemon juice

440g (14oz) canned black pitted cherries, drained

12 sheets filo pastry

125ml (4fl oz) melted butter

100g (3 1/2oz) ground almonds

icing sugar for garnish

1 Preheat oven to 190°C (375°F/ Gas 5). Place sugar, cinnamon and walnuts in a large bowl and mix well. Toss apple slices in lemon juice, then add with cherries to spice mixture and toss to coat.

2 Lay 1 sheet of filo on a flat surface, brush with butter and sprinkle with some of the almonds. Lay another filo sheet on top, brush with butter and sprinkle with almonds. Continue layering using remaining almonds and filo. Brush edges of the last sheet with butter.

3 Spoon fruit mixture along longest edge of pastry, 4cm (1 1/2in) from edge. Fold short sides in by about 3cm (1 1/2in), then roll the pastry up from the long end. Place strudel, seam-side-down, on paper-lined baking sheet and brush all over with some of the remaining butter.

4 Bake for 35-40 minutes, brushing with remaining butter if pastry starts to dry out. Cool 10 minutes on sheet before removing to a cooling rack. Dust with icing sugar and serve warm.

Serves 8

Mediterranean-Style Stuffed Peppers

Spanish Avocado Salad

2 avocados, stoned, peeled and thickly sliced crosswise

2 tblspn lemon juice

3 ripe tomatoes, peeled and thickly sliced

8 new baby potatoes, cooked and thickly sliced

1 green pepper, halved, blanched and cut into thick strips

8 black olives

125ml (4fl oz) Vinaigrette Dressing, see Tortellini Salad recipe page 30

lettuce leaves

1 small red onion, thinly sliced

1 Brush avocados with lemon juice to preserve colour.

2 Place tomatoes, potatoes, green pepper and olives in a bowl, add vinaigrette and lightly toss to combine. Arrange mixture in a serving bowl lined with lettuce leaves. Garnish with onion rings and avocado slices and serve.

Serves 6

Chinese Chicken Noodle Salad

375g (12oz) Chinese noodles

1 tblspn vegetable oil

500g (1lb) fresh bean sprouts

2 poached chicken breasts, shredded, see Crunchy Peach Chicken Salad recipe page 19

45g (1^1/$_2$oz) thinly sliced spring onions

toasted sesame seeds for garnish

Sesame Peanut Sauce

1 tspn chopped fresh ginger

1^1/$_2$ tblspn sesame oil

2^1/$_2$ tspn sugar

2 tblspn sesame seeds, toasted

1 tblspn groundnut (peanut) oil

4 tblspn peanut butter

4 tblspn water

2 tblspn soy sauce

2 tspn vinegar

^{1}/$_2$ tspn Tabasco sauce

^{1}/$_2$ tspn freshly ground black pepper

1 Cook noodles in a large saucepan of boiling salted water for 7 minutes or until tender. Drain, rinse under cold water, drain again and toss lightly with oil to prevent sticking. Place noodles in a serving bowl and top with bean sprouts, then shredded chicken.

2 To make sauce, place ginger, ^{1}/$_2$ tablespoon of the sesame oil and ^{1}/$_2$ teaspoon of the sugar in a small bowl, mix well and allow to stand for 30 minutes.

3 Place sesame seeds in a blender or food processor and process until crushed. Add ginger mixture with remaining ingredients and process until smooth.

4 Pour sauce over noodles, sprinkle with spring onions and garnish with sesame seeds. Toss well before serving.

Serves 4-6

Tomato and Bocconcini Salad

4 firm, ripe tomatoes

2 fresh baby mozzarella cheeses (bocconcini)

salt

freshly ground black pepper

3 tblspn olive oil

1 tspn lemon juice or wine vinegar

6-8 spring onions, chopped

8-10 fresh basil leaves, shredded

1 Using a serrated edged knife, cut tomatoes and cheeses crosswise into thin slices and arrange alternately overlapping on a flat dish. Season to taste with salt and black pepper .

2 Mix oil with lemon juice or vinegar and sprinkle over tomatoes. Blanch spring onions in boiling water for 30 seconds, refresh under cold water and drain well. Sprinkle onions and basil over salad before serving.

Serves 4

Clockwise from top: Spanish Avocado Salad, Tomato and Bocconcini Salad, Chinese Chicken Noodle Salad

Index

Managing Editor: Rachel Blackmore
Editors: Liz Goodman, Linda Venturoni
Production Manager: Sheridan Carter
Senior Production Editor: Anna Maguire
Production Editor: Sheridan Packer
Editorial and Production Assistant: Danielle Thiris
Layout and Finished Art: Stephen Joseph

Published by J.B. Fairfax Press Pty Limited
80-82 McLachlan Avenue
Rushcutters Bay, NSW 2011
A.C.N. 003 738 430

Formatted by J.B. Fairfax Press Pty Limited
Printed by Toppan Printing Co, Hong Kong
PRINTED IN HONG KONG

JBFP 379 A/UK
Includes Index
ISBN 1 86343 116 0 (set)
ISBN 1 86343 212 4

Distribution and Sales Enquiries
Australia: J.B. Fairfax Press Pty Limited
Ph: (02) 361 6366 Fax: (02) 360 6262
United Kingdom: J.B. Fairfax Press Limited
Ph: (0933) 402330 Fax: (0933) 402234